Nanny Goat's Boat

by Jane Belk Moncure
illustrated by Joy Friedman

Published by
THE CHILD'S WORLD ®

Mankato, Minnesota

GROLIER
B O O K S

Grolier Books is a division of
Grolier Enterprises, Inc.,
Danbury, CT.

The Library —
A Magic Castle

Come to the magic castle
When you are growing tall.
Rows upon rows of Word Windows
Line every single wall.
They reach up high,
As high as the sky,
And you want to open them all.
For every time you open one,
A new adventure has begun.

Andrew opened
a Word Window.
Here is what he read . . .

Nanny Goat had a boat,
a little sailboat.

"I will sail away,"
she said one day.

But the boat would not float.
And the goat lost her coat.

She was wet from her nose
to the tips of her toes.

Poor Goat soon had a very sore throat.

She went to the doctor. Guess what he said. "Take a pill, and stay in bed."

Her friends came to visit her, one at a time.

To cheer her up, each one came
with a rhyme.

The fox said, "Guess what is in this box.
Is it a tie,  or two pairs of socks?"

Goat said, "Socks. Thank-you, Fox."

Cat came with something in a hat.
"Is it a bird,  or a ball and a bat?"
asked Cat.

Goat said, "A ball and a bat. Thank-you, Cat."

Three butterflies came with a sweet surprise.
"Close your eyes," said the butterflies.

"Is this a book,

or a strawberry pie?"

Goat said, "Pie. Thank-you, Butterflies."

Two kangaroos
jumped up
the stairs.

"We brought you things that come in pairs.

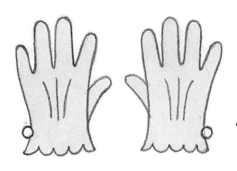 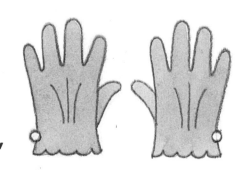

Two pairs of gloves,

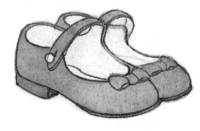 or two pairs of shoes?

Can you guess?"
asked the kangaroos.

Goat did.
Can you?

Ape came with a gift for Nanny Goat.

"This is to wear when you sail in your boat.

Is it a scarf,

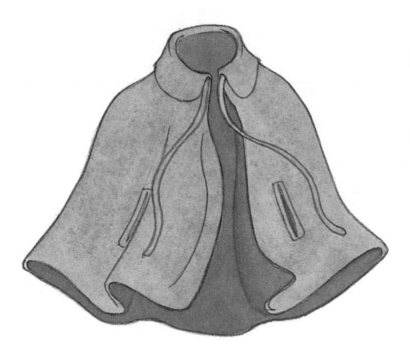

or a cape?"
asked the ape.

You know. Isn't that so?

Bear also gave Goat something to wear.

"Is it a dress,

or a bow for your hair?"
asked Bear.

Did Goat say, "A bow for my hair, Bear"?

Bunny gave Goat something funny.

"Is this a balloon,

or a bank full of money?" asked Bunny.

"Great!" said the goat. "I can buy
a new boat." She quickly got over
her bad sore throat.

Then she bought a new boat,
one that would float.

She wrote each friend a little note.

Thank you for rhyming
me a rhyme.
Come sailing with me
anytime.
You have been so nice
to me.
Come to my party at
half past three.

So Goat is giving a party. My, what a treat. Guess what? There is one empty seat. The seat is for you!

Goat says, "Rhyme me a rhyme
and come to my party anytime."

You can rhyme these rhymes with
Nanny Goat.

When she sailed with the fox,
    she wore her _____. socks

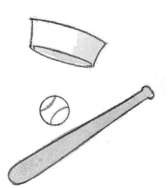

When she sailed with the cat,
    she wore her _____ hat
    and took her _____.

             ball and bat

When she sailed with the kangaroos,
    she wore her _____. shoes